NATIONAL STRATEGY FOR

# VICTORY
# IN IRAQ

NATIONAL SECURITY COUNCIL

NOVEMBER 2005

# Table of Contents

LOWER
SUWANNEE
NATIONAL
WILDLIFE
REFUGE

Comprehensive
Conservation
Plans

**LOWER SUWANNEE NATIONAL WILDLIFE REFUGE**

**Comprehensive Conservation Plans**

**LOWER SUWANNEE NATIONAL WILDLIFE REFUGE**

**Comprehensive Conservation Plans**

# INTRODUCTION

## Mission of the National Wildlife Refuge System

The mission of the National Wildlife Refuge System is to administer a national network of lands and waters for the conservation, management, and where appropriate, restoration of the fish, wildlife, and plant resources and their habitats within the United States for the benefit of present and future generations of Americans.

Skimmers
USFWS Ken Litzenberger

## Description of the Refuges

Located along the southern edge of the Big Bend Region of Florida's west coast, Lower Suwannee and Cedar Keys National Wildlife Refuges represent two jewels of the National Wildlife Refuge System (Fig. 2). Lower Suwannee National Wildlife Refuge was established on April 10, 1979, for the purpose of protecting, maintaining, and enhancing a rare and beautiful ecosystem. The refuge, which is predominantly wetlands, is bisected by 20 miles of Stephen Foster's famous Suwannee River and includes 20 miles of coastal marsh habitat along the Gulf coast. The salt marshes and tidal flats at the river's mouth are a paradise for shorebirds and fish. The refuge also encompasses an unusual diversity of floodplain hardwoods; cypress-lined sloughs; cabbage palm and cedar islands; cypress domes; hydric, mesic, and xeric hardwood hammocks; and low pine flatwoods.

Cedar Keys National Wildlife Refuge was established on July 16, 1929, to protect a breeding ground for colonial nesting migratory birds. Today, the refuge is comprised of 13 islands ranging in size from 1 to 120 acres and totaling 762 acres. Four of the islands, Snake, Seahorse, North and Deadman Keys, are designated Wilderness Areas. Additionally, Atsena Otie Key is state-owned and managed as part of Cedar Keys National Wildlife Refuge through a Memorandum of Understanding. Cedar Keys Refuge ranks as one of the largest nesting areas for colonial wading birds in north Florida.

Iris
USFWS Robert LeMarie

## Purpose of and Need for the Plan

Under the provisions of the National Wildlife Refuge System Improvement Act of 1997, the U. S. Fish and Wildlife Service is required to develop comprehensive conservation plans for all lands and waters of the National Wildlife Refuge System. These plans will guide management decisions and set forth strategies for achieving the purposes of each refuge unit. The National Environmental Policy Act ensures that the Service will assess the environmental impacts of any actions taken as a result of implementing these plans.

The following Comprehensive Conservation Plans and have been prepared for the Lower Suwannee and Cedar Keys National Wildlife Refuges, located in Levy and Dixie Counties, Florida. Their purposes are to identify the roles the refuges will play to support the mission of the National Wildlife Refuge System and the North Florida Ecosystem. The plans outline issues, concerns, and opportunities expressed to the Service during a series of public scoping meetings, workshops, and on comment sheets. They also provide a description of desired future conditions and propose long-range guidance to accomplish the purposes, missions, and visions of the refuges. This guidance is presented for each refuge in a listing of goals, objectives, and strategies resulting from an analysis of possible management alternatives.

The final plans will serve as operational guides for management of these refuges over the next 10 to 15 years.

### The plans will:

- provide a clear statement of the desired future conditions when refuge purposes and goals are accomplished;
- provide refuge neighbors and visitors with a clear understanding of the reasons for management actions on the refuge;
- ensure management of the refuge reflects policies and goals of the National Wildlife Refuge System;
- ensure refuge management is consistent with federal, state, and county plans;
- provide long-term continuity in refuge management; and
- provide a basis for operation, maintenance, and capital improvement budget requests.

River Trail Overlook
*USFWS ©Ken Sourbeer*

**Figure 1. Organizational Chart of the Fish and Wildlife Service within the U.S. Department of the Interior**

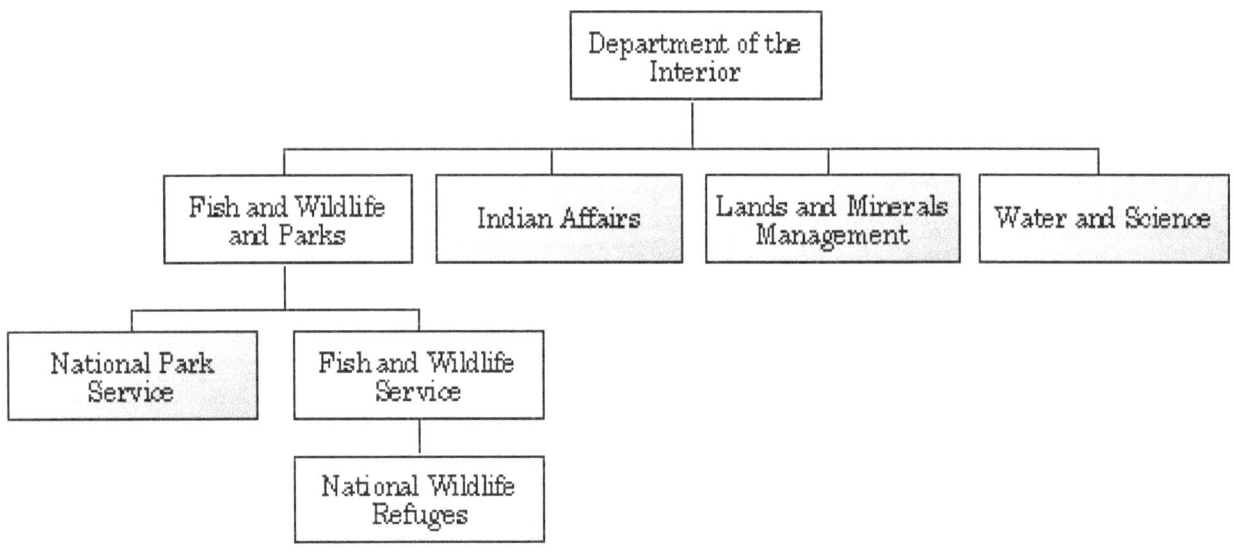

Swallow-tailed Kite
*USFWS ©Ken Myers*

Cypress Swamp
*USFWS ©Ken Sourbeer*

## Overview of the Department of the Interior

The Department of the Interior is the principal landowner of most of our nationally owned public lands and cultural resources. Management responsibilities include fostering wise use of our land and water resources, protecting our fish and wildlife, preserving the environmental and cultural values of our national parks and historical places, managing the National Wildlife Refuge System, and providing for the enjoyment of life through outdoor recreation (Fig. 1).

## Mission of the Fish and Wildlife Service

The Fish and Wildlife Service is the principal organization through which the Department of the Interior carries out its responsibilities of working with others to conserve, protect, and enhance the nation's fish and wildlife and their habitats for the continuing benefit of people.

The Service manages the National Wildlife Refuge System, the world's largest collection of lands set aside specifically for the protection of fish and wildlife populations and habitats. More than 520 national wildlife refuges covering more than 93 million acres provide important habitat for native plants and many species of insects, amphibians, reptiles, fish, birds, and mammals. These refuges also play a vital role in preserving threatened and endangered species, as well as offering a wide variety of recreational opportunities. Many refuges have visitor centers, wildlife trails, and environmental education programs. Nationwide, more than 30 million visitors annually hunt, fish, observe and photograph wildlife, or participate in interpretive activities on national wildlife refuges. The Service also manages all national fish hatcheries.

## Ecosystem Management and Priorities

For the Service, the North Florida Ecosystem includes portions of south Georgia and most of north and central Florida (Fig 2). The area includes southern temperate and subtropical climates, numerous physiographic districts, and many unique and widely varied habitat types. The northern boundary of this ecosystem includes the watersheds of the St. Mary's and Suwannee Rivers, including the Okefenokee Swamp. The northeast boundary begins at Camden County, Georgia, and proceeds down the east

**Figure 2. North Florida Ecosystem Map, Fish and Wildlife Service**

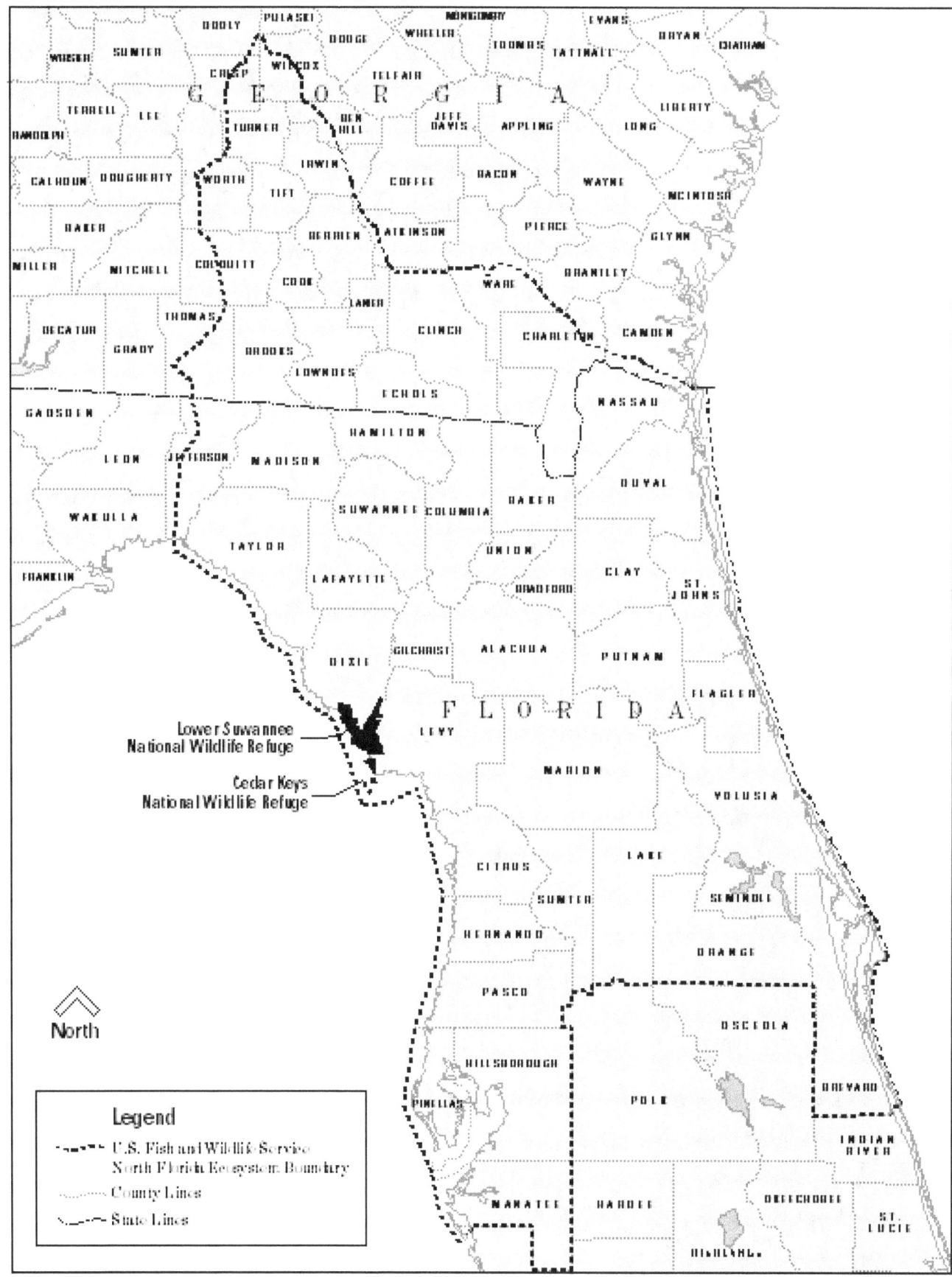

coast of Florida to the line separating Brevard and Indian River Counties. The ecosystem boundary then turns west and includes Orange, Lake, and Sumter Counties as its southern border. The western boundary includes all Florida counties from Sarasota north through Taylor and Jefferson Counties. In Georgia, the ecosystem is inclusive of all counties east and south of Thomas, Colquitt, Worth, Turner, Ben Hill, Coffee, Ware, Charlton, and Camden Counties.

Habitats found within this ecosystem include barrier islands; xeric scrub; pine flatwoods; freshwater marshes, lakes, streams and springs; mixed hardwood/pine forests; cypress swamps and domes; dry prairies; maritime forests; hardwood hammocks; estuarine marshes; pine rocklands; sandhill woodlands; coastal strands; sawgrass prairies; sloughs; and tree islands. The North Florida Ecosystem team currently has three priorities which include restoring scrub habitat, conserving coastal habitat, and protecting the water quality of the Suwannee River Basin.

### Legal Policy, Administrative Guidelines, and Other Considerations

Administration of national wildlife refuges is governed by various international treaties, federal laws, Presidential Executive Orders and regulations affecting land and water, as well as by the conservation and management of fish and wildlife resources. Policies for management options for the refuge are further refined by administrative guidelines established by the Secretary of the Interior and policy guidelines established by the Director of the Fish and Wildlife Service.

Select legal summaries of treaties and laws relevant to administration of the National Wildlife Refuge System and management of these refuges are provided in Appendix A.

Boat on River
*USFWS Allyne Askins*

*Planning Issues
and Opportunities*

### Overview of the Public Involvement Process

The Comprehensive Conservation Plans for Lower Suwannee and Cedar Keys National Wildlife Refuges have been prepared in compliance with the provisions of the National Wildlife Refuge System Improvement Act of 1997. Plan preparation is in compliance with the National Environmental Policy Act of 1969, which requires the Service to actively seek public involvement in the preparation of environmental assessments and environmental impact statements. It also requires the Service to seriously consider all reasonable alternatives, including a No Action Alternative and a Proposed Alternative. These alternatives are described in Environmental Assessements prepared in conjunction with the comprehension conservation plans for both Lower Suwannee and Cedar Keys Refuges.

CCP Planning Team
*USFWS Allyne Askins*

Identification of important issues provides a sound basis for initiating the development of management alternatives, objectives, and strategies. To ensure that the future management of these refuges reflects the issues, concerns, and opportunities expressed by the public, a variety of scoping mechanisms was used. A complete description of the public participation process during the draft and final plan preparation is included in Appendices B and D.

### Public Participation Highlights

- A comment packet was used to gather general information on current and potential refuge operations.
- Letters were mailed to affected and interested members of the public to inform them of the planning process and to invite their participation.
- Refuge personnel presented informative programs to community organizations and stakeholder groups.
- A series of stakeholder workshops and public scoping meetings were held to develop components of the draft plans.
- The draft plans were distributed to approximately 300 individuals, organizations, agencies, and Native American tribes.
- More than 80 participants attended a public meeting to discuss the draft plans.
- Both written and oral comments were received during a 60-day comment period.

## Scope of Issues, Concerns, and Opportunities

Several key issues and concerns surfaced during two public meetings, two stakeholder workshops, and from written comments. The planning team reviewed the issues and concerns raised by the approximately 100 people who participated in the scoping process. This list was based on the team's knowledge of the area, information gathered during the scoping meetings, and written comments submitted by the public.

CCP Planning Team
*USFWS Allyne Askins*

# Lower Suwannee
## *National Wildlife Refuge*

Aerial View of the Suwannee River
*USFWS Ken Litzenberger*

*Background
Information*

## Location

Located along the southern edge of the Big Bend Region of Florida's west coast, the Lower Suwannee National Wildlife Refuge is found in the westernmost part of Levy County and the southern tip of Dixie County (Fig. 3). The refuge is approximately 50 miles southwest of Gainesville, Florida.

## History

Lower Suwannee National Wildlife Refuge was established on April 10, 1979, under the authority of the Fish and Wildlife Act to protect the lower Suwannee River ecosystem. The initial acquisition in 1979 was 5,300 acres of land at Shired Island. Additional parcels of land were acquired over a 15-year period, until the refuge reached its present size of 52,935 acres. The refuge, which is predominantly wetlands, is bisected by 20 miles of Stephen Foster's famous Suwannee River and includes more than 20 miles of coastal marsh along the Gulf coast. The refuge also encompasses an unusual diversity of floodplain hardwoods; cypress-lined sloughs; cabbage palm and cedar islands; cypress domes; hydric, mesic, and xeric hardwood hammocks; and low pine flatwoods. Each of these diverse vegetative communities contributes to making Lower Suwannee National Wildlife Refuge one of the largest undeveloped river delta-estuarine systems in the United States.

Marsh
*USFWS ©Ken Sourbeer*

## Purpose

The purpose of Lower Suwannee National Wildlife Refuge is:
"...for the development, advancement, management, conservation, and protection of fish and wildlife resources...." 16 U.S.C. § 742f(a)(4)* and
"...for the benefit of the United States Fish and Wildlife Service, in performing its activities and services. Such acceptance may be subject to the terms of any restrictive or affirmative covenant, or condition of servitude...." 16 U.S.C. § 742f(b)(1) (Fish and Wildlife Act of 1956, 16 U.S.C. § 742f(a)-754, as amended.

Paddling the Refuge Canoe Trail
*USFWS Ken Litzenberger*

Lower Suwannee National Wildlife Refuge was established to protect, maintain, enhance, and where appropriate, restore habitats along the lower reaches of the Suwannee River. The refuge also protects water quality and quantity through sound land resource management and cooperative relationships with state agencies that have jurisdictional authority over the water and aquatic resources therein. Further, the refuge provides habitat for several threatened and endangered species and species of special concern in the State of Florida (Appendix H).

### Function within the Ecosystem

Lower Suwannee National Wildlife Refuge, along with Okefenokee National Wildlife Refuge, anchors the Suwannee River Basin - an area consisting of 10,000 square miles across two states. The primary focus of the Service in this ecosystem is to maintain the quality of large, undeveloped forested and wetland habitats in the upper and lower portions of the Suwannee River by linking those areas with a corridor of habitat along the river. The Service is also concerned with maintaining the quantity and quality of river flows and the rich biological heritage of the native plant species within the river basin. The refuge plays an integral role in meeting these ecosystem goals by protecting nearly 53,000 acres of riverine habitat and more than 20 miles of river corridor along the lower reaches of the Suwannee River.

### Agreements

■ Memorandum of Understanding with the Suwannee River Water Management District for management of its 420-acre St. Petersburg tract, as part of the Lower Suwannee National Wildlife Refuge.

■ Memorandum of Understanding that gives management authority of the 146-acre, Service-owned Canavan tract in Columbia County to the District. This property was a Farmers Home Administration property that the Service acquired and is adjacent to other property owned by the Suwannee River Water Management District.

■ Lease agreement with the State of Florida, Division of Lands, for the Service to manage 624 acres in T 12 S, R 11 E, Section 16, as part of the Lower Suwannee National Wildlife Refuge.

■ Lease agreement with The Nature Conservancy for the Service to manage the 786-acre, Conservancy-owned, Cummer tract, as part of the Lower Suwannee National Wildlife Refuge.

■ Lease agreement with the Dixie County Board of Commissioners for the Commissioners to maintain the Shired Island boat ramp.

■ Memorandum of Understanding between the Service and Levy County Sheriff's Department allowing either agency to provide emergency assistance to the other upon request.

■ Memorandum of Understanding between the Service and Dixie County Sheriff's Department allowing either agency to provide emergency assistance to the other upon request.

■ Memorandum of Understanding between the Service and the State of Florida, Department of Agricultural and Consumer Services, Division of Forestry, to provide wildfire suppression.

### Mission

*Management
Direction*

The mission of the Lower Suwannee National Wildlife Refuge is to protect, maintain, and enhance a significant natural ecosystem which encompasses flood plain hardwoods, coastal and freshwater marshes, and upland forests; provide optimum habitat conditions and protection for native wildlife with special emphasis on threatened and endangered species and migratory birds; provide wildlife-oriented recreational/educational opportunities to the public; and preserve significant archaeological sites.

Figure 3. Vicinity Map, Lower Suwannee National Wildlife Refuge

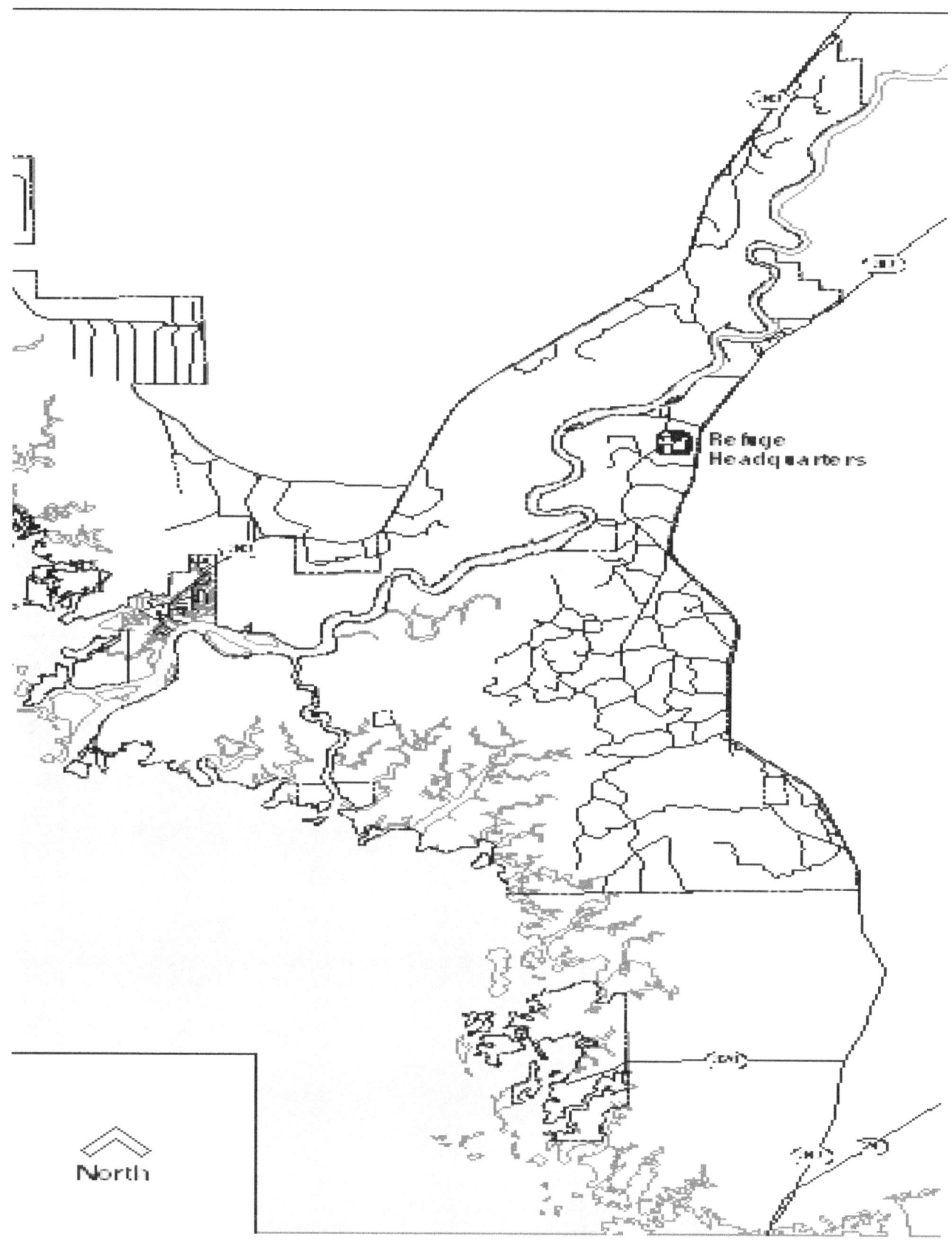

North

**LOWER
SUWANNEE
NATIONAL
WILDLIFE
REFUGE**

Comprehensive
Conservation
Plan

## Vision Statement

*The watershed and estuary of the Lower Suwannee National Wildlife Refuge contain valuable water resources and fish and wildlife habitat. The refuge will be managed for the conservation of fish and wildlife and their habitat, with special emphasis on the protection and restoration of wetland and upland communities. Education, research, and wildlife-dependent recreational opportunities will be available, insofar as they are compatible with refuge health and preservation. Management will partner with local, state and federal agencies; community organizations; and individuals to ensure the protection and conservation of the vast Suwannee River ecosystem for current and future generations.*

## Management Alternatives

Once the key issues and concerns were identified, the planning team determined a reasonable range of alternatives for managing the refuge. The Environmental Assessment, which is under a separate cover, contains a full review of the alternatives considered and their impacts on the socioeconomic, environmental, and cultural resources, along with alternatives discussed but not fully developed.

Birders on Canoe Trail
*USFWS Ken Litzenberger*

## Management Action

The management action was selected based on conformity with the refuge's mission, vision, ecosystem function, and current uses, as well as on the needs expressed by the public during the scoping process. The action will result in a better understanding of the refuge resources used by threatened and endangered species, migratory birds, and resident wildlife; the protection and enhancement of these resources; the protection of water quality and quantity; the restoration of refuge habitats; and accessibility of the refuge to the public for compatible wildlife-dependent public uses.

An overriding concern reflected in the plan is that wildlife comes first in refuge management. Public uses are allowed and encouraged if they are compatible with wildlife conservation. Wildlife-dependent recreational uses such as hunting, fishing, wildlife observation, wildlife photography, and environmental education and interpretation are emphasized.

The end result is a set of goals, objectives, and strategies related to key issues that will guide management of the refuge for the next 10 to 15 years.

LOWER
SUWANNEE
NATIONAL
WILDLIFE
REFUGE

Comprehensive
Conservation
Plan

## Goals, Objectives, and Strategies to Support the Management Action

Five management goals for Lower Suwannee National Wildlife Refuge were developed from several workshops held during the scoping process.

- **Wildlife** Expand scientifically based monitoring and research to support management decisions regarding wildlife habitat and populations.

- **Habitat** Restore, conserve, and enhance the natural diversity, abundance, and ecological function of refuge habitat, with an emphasis on managing habitat to benefit threatened and endangered species and species of special concern in the State of Florida.

- **Resource Protection** Protect the natural and cultural resources of the refuge to ensure their integrity and to fulfill the mission of the National Wildlife Refuge System.

- **Public Use** Provide opportunities for environmental education and interpretation and wildlife-dependent recreation in accordance with the National Wildlife Refuge System Improvement Act of 1997.

- **Landscape Management** Promote interagency and private landowner cooperation and partnerships for the management and protection of natural and cultural resources within the Big Bend Region of Florida, the Suwannee River Basin, and the North Florida Ecosystem to benefit wildlife, water quality and quantity, and the American people.

The goals, objectives, and strategies are the Service's response to the issues and concerns expressed by the planning team and the general public at the workshops, public meetings, and in the comment packet, and will be used to implement the management action. These goals, objectives, and strategies reflect the refuges's commitment to achieving the missions of the Service and of the National Wildlife Refuge System; ecosystem priorities; refuge purposes, mission and vision; and the expressed needs of the public—provided that necessary funding requirements are met.

Snapping Turtle
*USFWS Ken Litaenberger*

### Wildlife
*Goal*

1.  Expand scientifically based monitoring and research to support management decisions regarding wildlife habitat and populations.

    *Objective*

    1.1  Conduct surveys of vertebrates, invertebrates, and plant species and habitat associations; develop monitoring programs for priority species; and establish targets for population levels. Expand current monitoring programs.

    *Strategies*

    1.1.1  Continue current monitoring program for bald eagles during the nesting season using aerial surveys to determine nest status and production. Provide data to the Florida Fish and Wildlife Conservation Commission and the Service to aid in monitoring the delisting of this species.

    1.1.2  Continue current monitoring program during the osprey nesting season to determine fledgling success and to evaluate overall population trends.

    1.1.3  Expand the current, sporadic monitoring program for manatees into a regular, consistent monitoring program using aerial surveys of the coastal and riverine habitats of the refuge. Provide data to the Service Manatee Recovery Coordinator to aid in statewide monitoring and recovery efforts.

Youth Hunting
*USFWS*

Great Blue Heron
*USFWS ©Bruce Colin*

Alligator
*USFWS ©Bruce Colin*

1.1.4 Continue to support the U.S. Geological Survey and the Service's efforts to monitor threatened Gulf sturgeon that use the Suwannee River and coastal estuary. Provide assistance for storage, transporting, and setting up equipment. Assist in field research as needed.

1.1.5 Continue monitoring the population status and health of resident wildlife species (e.g., white-tailed deer and wild turkey) and tailor management activities and hunting regulations to maintain healthy and stable populations of game species. Use Southeastern Cooperative Disease Study Unit at the University of Georgia to monitor health of deer herd on a 5-year basis.

1.1.6 By 2001, develop and implement an annual Breeding Bird Survey.

1.1.7 By 2001, participate in migratory shore bird surveys in spring and fall and provide data to the Manomet Laboratory.

1.1.8 By 2002, conduct a population survey of gopher tortoises and their habitat associations. Trap five tortoises and conduct blood tests to determine if the population harbors the respiratory disease which threatens this species. Beginning in 2005, monitor gopher tortoise populations every 5 years to determine long-term population trends. (Resource Project 4)

1.1.9 By 2003, conduct furbearer counts, determine their effects on the ecosystem, and develop population management strategies (e.g., hunting and trapping) to promote diversity and stability among species and their habitats.

1.1.10 By 2003, initiate a nesting survey of swallow-tailed kites to be conducted every 5 years to determine long-term population trends.

1.1.11 By 2004, identify exotic plant and animal species on the refuge and develop a strategy to eliminate or control them.

1.1.12 By 2005, partner with the University of Florida to conduct a survey of herpetofauna and develop a long-term monitoring technique for amphibians.

1.1.13 By 2005, partner with the Suwannee River Water Management District and/or the U.S. Geological Survey to conduct an aquatic inventory of fishes and mussels of the lower reaches of the Suwannee River.

1.1.14 By 2008, develop a list of significant flora and conduct surveys for rare and endangered plant species.

*Objectives*

1.2 By 2004, revise the Wildlife Inventory Plan into a Wildlife Management Plan which would be based on data gathered during initial surveys. The Wildlife Management Plan would guide all aspects of refuge management and be based on reliable data and sound techniques.

LOWER
SUWANNEE
NATIONAL
WILDLIFE
REFUGE

Comprehensive
Conservation
Plan

Pine Lily
*USFWS Robert LeMarie*

1.3    By 2010, conduct a biological review of the refuge. Ideally, this review would have occurred prior to the initiation of this comprehensive conservation plan. It will be necessary to conduct a biological review prior to its revision to determine if biological strategies outlined in the plan and in the Wildlife Management Plan are resulting in good science and sound management practices.

1.4    Develop a Geographic Information System database management and mapping system with plant and wildlife communities and management layers. (Resource Project 7).

*Strategies*

1.4.1    By 2003, develop a computerized database for current and past monitoring and research activities using Microsoft Access and input all available records.

1.4.2    By 2003, develop a computerized database for current and past forestry and fire activities using Microsoft Access and input all available records.

1.4.3    By 2003, maintain database and develop a query system to facilitate data retrieval.

1.4.4    By 2004, train professional staff in data collection and usage of Geographic Information System.

1.4.5    By 2006, build Geographic Information System databases with several coverages including: roads; land cover types; prescribed burn units; timber sales; inholdings; hydrology; soils; wildfires; boundary maintenance; boundaries; breeding bird survey transects; data points and data; eagle nests; osprey nests; gopher tortoise burrows; gopher tortoise study transects; archaeological and cultural sites; topography; assets (structures and facilities); public use structures and trails; swallow-tailed kite nests; forest compartments and stands; insect/disease/ disturbance events; beaver ponds and dams; refuge ponds; blue bird boxes; and wood duck boxes.

## Habitat
*Goal*

2.    Restore, conserve, and enhance the natural diversity, abundance, and ecological function of refuge habitats, with an emphasis on managing habitat to benefit threatened and endangered species and species of special concern in the State of Florida.

*Objective*

2.1    Maintain habitat for migrating, wintering, nesting, and foraging birds, with special emphasis on threatened and endangered species, neotropical migratory birds, and colonial wading birds.

*Strategies*

2.1.1    Maintain existing pine and hardwood habitat for at least 20 pairs of swallow-tailed kites.

2.1.2    Maintain existing nesting habitat for 4 pairs of bald eagles.

2.1.3    Maintain existing habitat for 30 to 40 nesting pairs of osprey.

2.1.4    Provide high quality foraging habitat for colonial

LOWER
SUWANNEE
NATIONAL
WILDLIFE
REFUGE

Comprehensive
Conservation
Plan

Marsh Burning
*USFWS Ken Litzenberger*

Planting Trees
*USFWS Ken Litzenberger*

Logging Deck
*USFWS Ken Litzenberger*

wading birds by manipulating water levels in three existing management areas.

2.1.5 By 2002, initiate a research project with the Service's Ecological Services Division, the University of Florida, and the Suwannee River Water Management District to study mercury levels in the river and its tributaries and the effects on foraging wading birds.

*Objective*

2.2 Refine and implement a prescribed fire program to restore and maintain healthy, fire-dependent communities.

*Strategies*

2.2.1 Implement the Fire Management Plan (1997), with annual reviews and updates to incorporate applied research findings.

2.2.2 Continue on an annual basis to use prescribed fire on at least 3,000 acres, using a combination of dormant season and growing season burns. Both uplands and marshlands will be burned.

2.2.3 By the 2003 fire season, initiate fire research on the effects of burning frequency, seasonality, and spatial distribution on the refuge's pine flatwoods, mixed cypress, and marsh ecosystems. (Resource Project 5)

2.2.4 By 2004, investigate the impacts of prescribed fire on isolated wetlands in relation to restoring and maintaining aquatic habitats for herpetofauna threatened by hardwood succession caused by the exclusion of fire. (Resource Project 5)

*Objective*

2.3 Refine and implement an active forest management program to restore and maintain healthy and diverse forest communities.

*Strategies*

2.3.1 Plant wiregrass plugs in the longleaf pine restoration sites and log decks at a density of 1,000-per-acre with an annual average restoration of 10 acres.

2.3.2 Maintain and promote propagation of wiregrass through prescribed fire.

2.3.3 In 2001, monitor restoration efforts of native long leaf pine and wiregrass communities on slash pine conversion sites (clearcuts). Conduct seedling survival counts in the restoration areas to determine survival rate.

2.3.4 By 2002, update and implement the Forest Management Plan (1989).

2.3.5 By 2002, complete inventory preparations for the forested habitats, including inventory schedules, data to be collected, preparation of cruise maps based on refuge management compartment maps, and methods for analyzing data.

2.3.6 In 2002, begin inventory of the 32,571 acres of forested habitats to obtain the necessary data to

LOWER
SUWANNEE
NATIONAL
WILDLIFE
REFUGE

Comprehensive
Conservation
Plan

refine forest and wildlife management strategies. A minimum of 3,000 acres will be inventoried annually. Complete the inventory project in 2011, followed by the necessary revisions to the Forest Management Plan.

2.3.7 Use commercial timber sales to thin slash pine plantations to promote the regeneration of early successional understories, provide quality habitat and forage for native wildlife species, and prepare plantations for a shift to growing season fires. Specific harvest schedules will be developed in the Forest Management Plan.

2.3.8 Monitor and evaluate the wiregrass restoration effort and determine if the project should continue past 2004.

2.3.9 If adequate, wiregrass stands could be used as a seed source. Implement a seed harvest program to expand the restoration process, if previous restoration efforts are successful.

*Objective*

2.4 Protect wildlife habitat and water quality and quantity through land acquisition. (Resource Project 3)

*Strategies*

2.4.1 Protect important habitat for threatened Gulf sturgeon and water quality of the Suwanee River by acquiring, through fee title ownership or easements, the tracts identified in the *Environmental Assessment and Land Protection Plan for the Expansion of the Lower Suwannee National Wildlife Refuge (1995).*

2.4.2 Protect and restore Florida scrub jay habitat and provide contiguous habitat for numerous other species through the acquisition of the Caber Tract, if this land becomes available for purchase.

2.4.3 Acquire the 17 remaining privately owned properties (inholdings) within the original approved acquisition boundary of the refuge, as they become available for purchase.

## Resource Protection

*Goal*

3. Protect the natural and cultural resources of the refuge to ensure their integrity and to fulfill the mission of the National Wildlife Refuge System.

*Objective*

3.1 Protect known archaeological and historical sites on the refuge from illegal take or damage in compliance with the Archaeological Resources Protection Act, the Native American Graves Protection and Repatriation Act, and the National Historic Preservation Act.

*Strategies*

3.1.1 Conduct law enforcement patrols at all known archaeological and historical sites on a regular basis to inspect for disturbance and illegal digging and/or looting.

Pine Forest
*USFWS ©Ken Sourbeer*

LOWER
SUWANNEE
NATIONAL
WILDLIFE
REFUGE

Comprehensive
Conservation
Plan

Grading Roads
*USFWS Ken Litzenberger*

Shired Creek Bridge
*USFWS Ken Litzenberger*

3.1.2 By 2003, compile a comprehensive literature review of past archaeological, anthropological, and historical investigations within and near the refuge. Produce an annotated bibliography to document the area's history.

3.1.3 By 2006, inventory and GPS the refuge's archaeological sites. (Resource Projects 7 and 14)

3.1.4 By 2010, develop and implement a plan to protect identified archaeological sites in consultation with the Service's Archaeologist, the State Historic Preservation Office, Native American tribes, and the professional archaeological community. (Resource Project 14)

*Objectives*

3.2 Annually evaluate a minimum of 15 miles of refuge boundary. Delineate refuge boundaries with signs and paint, as needed.

3.3 Continue to protect refuge habitats from wildfire through the fire program, properly trained staff, and equipment readiness. The station will monitor fire conditions and respond according to approved plans and procedures.

3.4 Continue to protect bald eagle nests by monitoring for disturbance and, if necessary, by closing areas around nests during the nesting season.

3.5 Continue to provide visitor safety, protect resources, and ensure compliance with refuge regulations for more than 100,000 annual visitors through law enforcement patrols and public use contacts.

*Strategy*

3.5.1 By 2005, revise and update the refuge's Law Enforcement Plan.

*Objectives*

3.6 Continue to work cooperatively with local, state, and other federal law enforcement agencies to enhance resource protection.

3.7 Maintain present road system containing 50 miles of primary refuge roads by grading, mowing, and replacing culverts, as needed, for public vehicle access and for habitat improvement, protection, and management.

3.8 Maintain access to secondary roads system by mowing, boom axing, grading, and replacing culverts, as needed, for habitat protection, management, and improvement for refuge staff and for public foot and bicycle traffic.

3.9 Identify additional lands and seek funding to acquire such lands that will improve resource protection and aid in fulfilling the mission and purpose of the refuge.

3.10 Maintain more than $1,000,000 worth of capitalized equipment used in all aspects of refuge management including habitat, wildlife, and public use.

LOWER
SUWANNEE
NATIONAL
WILDLIFE
REFUGE

Comprehensive
Conservation
Plan

3.11 By 2006, conduct a wilderness review of the refuge. The purpose of a wilderness review is to determine whether any refuge lands or waters meet the characteristics of wilderness. Any lands determined to meet these criteria will then be nominated for inclusion as Wilderness Areas.

### Public Use
*Goal*

4. Provide opportunities for environmental education and interpretation and wildlife-dependent recreation in accordance with the National Wildlife Refuge System Improvement Act of 1997.

*Objectives*

4.1 By 2003, develop and implement a Visitor Services Management Plan.

4.2 By 2002, identify site for a visitor center or visitor contact station to serve both Lower Suwannee and Cedar Keys National Wildlife Refuges. Visitors will learn about the Service, the National Wildlife Refuge System, and both local refuges and the trust resources they protect. Seek funding support from Congressional representatives, local governments, organizations, and individuals. (Resource Project 2)

4.3 Develop and implement an environmental education program that will result in a greater understanding and appreciation of refuge flora, fauna, and habitats.

*Strategies*

4.3.1 By 2001, quarterly provide ranger- or volunteer-led canoe tours, wildflower and butterfly walks, and birding trips.

4.3.2 By 2002, develop environmental education curriculum for the refuge consistent with Florida Department of Education (Sunshine State) standards.

4.3.3 By 2002, develop at least three refuge specific messages, complete with a teacher's guide on wetlands and wetlands species for local teachers and community organizations.

4.3.4 By 2003, develop teacher workshop materials and host an annual teacher's workshop for environmental education curriculum.

4.3.5 Provide and train staff, student interns, and community volunteers to implement an environmental education program. By 2003, increase staff and volunteer presence in the public schools and the community for educational purposes.

4.3.6 By 2005, provide temporary housing and transportation for student interns.

*Objective*

4.4 Update existing materials and develop new interpretive materials, including brochures, interpretive panels, kiosks, and exhibits that highlight refuge resources.

Cub Scouts
*USFWS Allyne Askins*

Fishbone Creek Observation Tower
*USFWS Ken Litaenberger*

**LOWER
SUWANNEE
NATIONAL
WILDLIFE
REFUGE**

Comprehensive
Conservation
Plan

*Strategies*

4.4.1 By 2001, replace temporary marsh walkways with elevated, accessible boardwalks. To provide resting spots, place benches along the trail. (Resource Project 9)

4.4.2 By 2001, develop interpretive panels which highlight the Dixie County portion of the refuge. The panels will be included on kiosks located near the refuge, on property owned by the county and town of Suwannee.

4.4.3 By 2002, develop a self-guided walking trail through the pine forests and marsh at Salt Creek.

4.4.4 By 2002, replace visitor's kiosk at River Trail with a new structure, panels, and brochure box. (Resource Project 8)

4.4.5 By 2003, develop interpretive panels and build a kiosk at the Shell Mound Unit. Interpretive panels will highlight coastal habitat and associated wildlife. A map will be included to identify refuge lands and public use facilities. (Resource Project 9)

4.4.6 By 2003, construct an observation tower at Dennis Creek Landing similar to the tower/disability accessible deck on the River Trail. (Resource Project 9)

4.4.7 By 2004, establish a native plants, wildflower, and butterfly garden at the refuge headquarters. Through interpretive signs and an accompanying guide, the area would become an outdoor classroom and serve as a demonstration area for "Backyard Wildlife Management."

4.4.8 By 2005, develop interpretive panels and incorporate into kiosks for the Dennis Creek and Shell Mound trails similar to those found along the River Trail. (Resource Project 9)

4.4.9 By 2006, construct an observation tower with interpretive panels overlooking an interior freshwater marsh/pond along the visitor loop road in Levy County.

Hunter
*USFWS Ken Litzenberger*

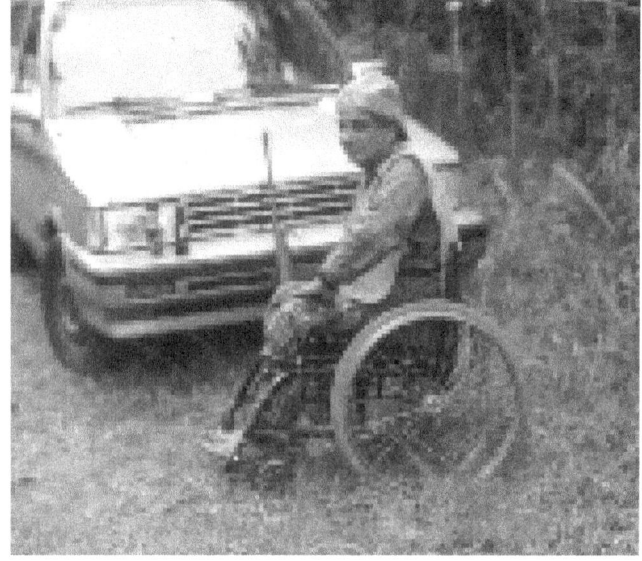

4.4.10 Evaluate other areas where walking trails for wildlife observation might be compatible with the purpose and mission of the refuge or refuge system.

*Objective*

4.5 Provide opportunities for hunting and fishing on the refuge in a manner which minimizes conflicts between consumptive and non-consumptive user groups.

*Strategies*

4.5.1 Provide high quality hunting opportunities for small game, big game, and waterfowl consistent with sound biological principles and in accordance with the approved Refuge Hunt Plan (1988).

LOWER
SUWANNEE
NATIONAL
WILDLIFE
REFUGE

Comprehensive
Conservation
Plan

Mother and Son Fishing
*USFWS Ken Litaenberger*

Fishing at Shell Mound Pier
*USFWS Ken Litzenberger*

Volunteer with Children
*USFWS Ken Litaenberger*

4.5.1.1   Maintain the archery-only area in Dixie County.

4.5.1.2   Continue to staff a centralized check station in each county during the general gun season to collect harvest data and provide a hunter contact point.

4.5.1.3   Continue to monitor and evaluate the hunt program annually to determine health of game species. Modify seasons and/or regulations, if necessary, to ensure the hunt program is based on sound biological information and achieving management goals.

4.5.1.4   By 2001, increase law enforcement presence during hunting seasons to ensure hunter safety, to provide contact information, and to monitor compliance.

4.5.1.5   By 2002, designate non-hunting areas in both counties to minimize potential conflicts between hunters and non-hunters. Potential areas to be included are the property owned by The Nature Conservancy, Shell Mound, Fishbone Creek, and Shired Island. These areas have public use facilities (e.g., trails and boardwalks).

4.5.1.6   By 2002, modify deer hunting regulations to increase the number of does harvested. This will achieve a balanced sex ratio and improve overall deer herd health.

4.5.1.7   By 2003, evaluate the potential of conducting a youth-oriented deer hunt.

4.5.2   Provide high quality fishing opportunities consistent with sound biological principles.

4.5.2.1   By 2001, increase law enforcement patrol of fishing areas to ensure public safety and maintain refurbished facilities.

4.5.2.2   By 2002, construct a disability-accessible fishing platform at Fishbone Creek.

4.5.2.3   By 2004, repair boat launch and resurface parking area at Shired Island. (Resource Project 12)

4.5.2.4   By 2005, explore additional ways to increase land based fishing opportunities by emphasizing access and facility improvements.

4.5.2.5   By 2006, develop and implement a fisheries management plan.

4.5.2.6   By 2008, support National Fishing Week by conducting an annual event.

**LOWER
SUWANNEE
NATIONAL
WILDLIFE
REFUGE**

Comprehensive
Conservation
Plan

Stugeon Capture
*USFWS Jim Clugston*

Lily Pads
*USFWS ©Bruce Colin*

*Objective*

4.6    Develop a volunteer program which offers resource, educational, and maintenance projects to accommodate a diverse volunteer community.

*Strategies*

4.6.1    Create partnerships with community-based organizations to adopt specific refuge trails and/or areas.

4.6.1.1    Continue coordinating with the Wetlands Clubs from area high schools to conduct regular clean-up days on the refuge.

4.6.1.2    By 2002, partner with the Suwannee River Chamber of Commerce to adopt the Dixie Mainline Trail.

4.6.2    Provide volunteer training opportunities.

4.6.2.1    Continue to provide training to teach refuge volunteers about the Service, the refuge system, and the local refuges.

4.6.2.2    By 2002, provide opportunities for volunteers to attend teacher workshops to develop skills for conducting educational programs.

4.6.2.3    By 2003, provide opportunities for volunteers to attend Service-sponsored training on related topics to improve their ability to serve refuge needs.

4.6.3    By 2001, provide support and recognition to volunteers for their contributions to refuge operations and programs.

4.6.4    By 2003, develop volunteer-led tours of various refuge trails.

4.6.5    By 2004, use volunteers to assist with staffing needs for the new refuge visitor center or contact station.

*Objective*

4.7    By 2001, develop a Friends Group for Lower Suwannee and Cedar Keys National Wildlife Refuges.

## Landscape Management

*Goal*

5.    Promote interagency and private landowner cooperation and partnerships for the management and protection of natural and cultural resources within the Big Bend Region of Florida, the Suwannee River Basin, and the North Florida Ecosystem to benefit wildlife, water quality and quantity, and the American people.

*Objectives*

5.1    Continue participation on North Florida Ecosystem Team and support team priorities and projects.

Bicyclists on the Dixie Mainline
*USFWS*

5.2    By 2005, develop partnerships with local school districts and state environmental agencies such as the Suwannee River Water Management District, Florida Department of Environmental Protection, and Florida Fish and Wildlife Conservation Commission to promote and provide environmental education opportunities on and off the refuge.

*Strategies*

5.2.1    By 2003, expand partnership with the Levy County School District to include it as an involved participant in the Interdisciplinary Watershed Education Program.

5.2.2    By 2004, expand partnership with the Dixie County School District to assist with the development of environmental education facilities and programs. (Resource Project 10)

*Objective*

5.3    By 2006, develop partnerships to protect water quality and quantity and to promote research on the trust resources of the refuge.

*Strategies*

5.3.1    By 2002, expand partnership with the University of Florida to conduct research on the refuge and provide research sites and field experiences to students.

5.3.2    By 2002, expand partnership with the Suwannee River Water Management District and the U.S. Geological Survey to include monitoring water flows and quality in the lower reaches of the Suwannee River, to inventory and study aquatic species, and to protect the Suwannee River corridor from development and activities which could negatively impact water quantity and quality.

5.3.3    By 2003, explore potential for working with the Florida Fish and Wildlife Conservation Commission to reintroduce black bear into the Big Bend Region of Florida.

5.3.4    Conduct a basin-wide mussel survey to determine species abundance and distribution with emphasis on determining status of the Suwannee moccasinshell mussel for possible listing, by the year 2005. Threats to the Suwannee River Basin include degradation of water quality resulting from increased pesticide and fertilizer use by dairy and poultry operations, contaminants from phosphate mines and pulp mills, and increased ground and surface water consumption (specifically, a proposal to divert water from the Suwannee River to the Tampa area [minimum flows issue]).

*Objective*

5.4    Maintain partnerships with local community organizations and environmental agencies to promote and guide the development of nature-based tourism while maintaining the "wildlife first" requirement of the Refuge Improvement Act.

LOWER
SUWANNEE
NATIONAL
WILDLIFE
REFUGE

Comprehensive
Conservation
Plan

*Strategies*

5.4.1 Continue to work with the Florida Park Service and other governmental agencies, as well as community organizations, in the sponsorship of the Suwannee River Naturefest, an annual nature-based festival.

5.4.2 Continue to partner with local organizations to seek out and apply for grants on collaborative projects.

5.4.3 By 2002, work with the Suwannee River and Dixie County Chambers of Commerce to develop interpretive material about the Dixie County portion of the refuge and nature-based recreation opportunities provided by the refuge.

5.4.4 By 2003, seek support from community organizations and governmental agencies for the establishment of a Refuge Visitor and Education Center which will serve both refuges and could serve as a central information point for environmental activities in the area.

*Objectives*

5.5 Continue to develop partnerships with national and state organizations to acquire necessary lands for the protection of trust resources and the fulfillment of the purpose and mission of the refuge.

5.6 Seek mutual cooperation with recognized Native American tribes in Florida to protect Native American sites on the refuge.

*Strategy*

5.6.1 By 2003, negotiate and implement a long-term archaeological research agreement with the Department of Anthropology at the University of Florida and the Museum of Natural History.

## Partnerships

*Plan Implementation*

A crucial component to implementing this comprehensive conservation plan is the development and expansion of partnerships with the local community and other environmental agencies. Significant partnerships with the Suwannee River Water Management District and The Nature Conservancy contributed to both the establishment and management of the refuge. Local organizations that have contributed to the operation of the refuge include the Suwannee River and Dixie County Chambers of Commerce, the Suwannee Audubon Society, and the "Save Our Suwannee" organization. Personal contacts and working relationships have been established with other governmental organizations including the following: University of Florida; Florida Fish and Wildlife Conservation Commission; Florida Park Service; Florida Department of Environmental Protection; Florida Division of Forestry; Levy County School District; Dixie County School District; Chiefland City Council; Levy County Commissioners; Dixie County Commissioners; Levy County Development Authority; North Florida Economic Development Council; Levy County Economic Development Council; and North Central Florida Regional Planning Council.

In addition to dynamic partnerships with organizations, the refuge is fortunate to have a small but dedicated group of individuals who volunteer and assist the refuge with various projects. These volunteers will continue to play a pivotal role in the accomplishment of refuge objectives and

Swamp Lily
*USFWS Robert LeMarie*

Water Snake
*USFWS ©Bruce Colin*

strategies. In addition to assisting with refuge projects, this cadre of volunteers serves as an important link with the community at large, promoting refuge messages and garnering additional support for the refuge system.

Partnerships with other environmental agencies, local school districts, and community groups have the greatest potential to benefit refuge resources. Biological and environmental research and monitoring will be improved through enhanced partnerships with the Suwannee River Water Management District, the University of Florida, and the Florida Fish and Wildlife Conservation Commission. Environmental education opportunities will be enhanced through expanded partnerships with both local school districts, the Suwannee River Water Management District and the Florida Fish and Wildlife Conservation Commission. The limiting factor in the advancement of these partnerships is the lack of staffing and funding to nurture these programs and relationships.

## Annual Work Plans

Future annual work plans will be developed to reflect the priorities and intent of this comprehensive conservation plan. When discretionary funding and staff time are available, these work plans will be used to implement various components of the plan.

## Step-Down Management Plans

The comprehensive conservation plan provides conceptual guidance for potential future expansion, management and development of the refuge. Step-down management plans are individual, subject-specific plans. Examples are fire management, forestry management and hunting management. The refuge's approved step-down plans are listed below. Before implementing the goals and projects of this comprehensive conservation plan, some specific step-down plans may need revisions, while others will need to be developed.

### *Approved Plans*

- **Aircraft Pre-Accident** Aircraft are used for fire control and management, habitat monitoring, and biological surveys. The purpose of the Aircraft Pre-Accident Plan is to outline general procedures to be followed during routine flights and flight emergencies. (Approved 5/6/94)

- **Continuity of Operations** It is important to maintain the capability to perform essential activities and functions under all circumstances and situations, including human-caused, natural, technological, and national security emergencies that may occur with or without notice. This plan identifies functions necessary for the safety and continuity of operations. (Written 8/10/98)

- **Fire Management** The purpose of the Fire Management Plan is to provide objectives and guidelines for managing refuge habitat. The plan provides a detailed program of action to implement fire management policies and objectives in accordance with the Fire Management Preparedness Handbook (621 FW). (Approved 1/8/97)

- **Hurricane Action** The purpose of the Hurricane Action Plan is to outline general procedures to be followed during and after hurricanes and the associated tornadoes which may occur. (Approved 12/17/90)

- **Station Safety** The purpose of the Station Safety and Environmental Health Management Plan is to outline responsibilities and procedures necessary to minimize accidents/incidents which may result in personal injury or property damage to Service employees and the visiting public. Included are guidelines for employees to follow in case of emergencies, correct procedures for reporting accidents, and an emergency action directory. (Approved 10/21/84)

Visitors at Shell Mount
*USFWS ©Ken Sourbeer*

**LOWER
SUWANNEE
NATIONAL
WILDLIFE
REFUGE**

Comprehensive
Conservation
Plan

■**Trapping** The purpose of this plan is to identify methods to reduce beaver impacts on refuge roads and timber in the Dixie County portion of the refuge. The plan does not seek to eliminate beaver from the refuge, merely minimize damage caused to refuge roads and timber by flooding, and thus ensure visitor and staff safety when using these roads. (Submitted 1/12/00)

## Approved Plans, Scheduled for Revisions

■**Forest Management** The purpose of this plan is to provide guidelines which will strive to make the best use of available management techniques to provide suitable habitat for native wildlife in refuge forest lands. This plan is scheduled to be updated by 2002. (Approved 4/19/89)

■**Law Enforcement** This plan's purpose is to provide refuge staff with a ready reference to Service, regional and state policies, procedures, and programs concerning refuge law enforcement activities. The present plan was approved on March 29, 1988, and is outdated. It will be revised by 2005.

■ **Visitor Services Management Plan (Public Use Management Plan)** The purpose of the Public Use Management Plan, now referred to as the Visitor Services Management Plan, is to outline strategies to accomplish the refuge's public use goals without compromising the original purpose for which the refuge was established. The plan will be revised in 2003. (Approved 6/28/88)

> ■ **Hunting** The purpose of the Hunting Plan is to establish guidelines for hunting on the refuge which will provide the general public with a quality wildlife-oriented recreational experience, an opportunity to utilize a renewable resource, and the ability to maintain wildlife populations at levels compatible with refuge habitat. This plan will be updated and incorporated into the Visitor Services Management Plan by the 2003-2004 hunt season. (Approved 4/18/88)

> ■ **Fishing** The purpose of the Fishing Plan is to provide guidelines and objectives for the sportfishing program, which will serve to increase wildlife-dependent recreational opportunities and further the public's opportunity to enjoy a renewable resource. The plan will be updated and included in the Visitor Services Management Plan, which is scheduled to be updated and revised by 2003. (Approved 8/16/88)

> ■ **Sign (part of Public Use Management Plan)** The sign plan, which is now obsolete, outlined the design and placement of refuge signs to provide information to the public. Sign management will now be included in the Visitor Services Management Plan. (Approved 6/28/88)

■ **Wildlife Management Plan (Wildlife Inventory Plan)** The purpose of the Wildlife Inventory Plan was to establish which species to inventory, standard techniques for conducting the inventories, and projected costs. This plan is now obsolete. A new Wildlife Management Plan will be written to replace this plan. This project is to be conducted by 2004. (Approved 4/21/86)

## Needed Plans or Reviews

■ **Cultural Resource Management Plan** The purpose of this plan is to clearly delineate the historic preservation process for the refuge, develop strategies to identify and assess the refuge's historic properties, identify appropriate site protection measures, and identify current and potential partners. The plan shall be in place by 2010.

■ **Wilderness Review** The purpose of this review is to determine whether any refuge lands or waters meet the qualifications of a "Wilderness Area." Any areas determined to meet these criteria will then be nominated for inclusion as wilderness. The Wilderness Review will be conducted by 2006.

River Trail Kiosk
*USFWS ©Ken Sourbeer*

Cypress Swamp
*USFWS ©Ken Sourbeer*

■ **Fisheries Management Plan** The purpose of this plan is to determine if and what management actions could be conducted to improve fish habitat on refuge waters. Fisheries biologists from the Service's Ecological Field Offices would provide the expertise needed for this evaluation. The fisheries plan will be conducted by 2006.

■ **Biological Review** Ideally, this review would have occurred prior to the initiation of this comprehensive conservation plan. It will be necessary to conduct a biological review prior to its revision to determine if biological strategies outlined in this plan and the Wildlife Management Plan are resulting in good science and sound management practices. This review should occur by 2010.

## Funding and Staffing

To bring the vision of the Lower Suwannee National Wildlife Refuge to a reality—expanded biological monitoring, enhanced public use opportunities, and construction of related facilities—*appropriate funding and staffing are essential!* Although a portion of this new funding could be from partnership opportunities and grants, the bulk of the funding must be allocated by the U.S. Congress. Current base funding is inadequate to meet staff costs and to complete routine maintenance and upkeep of facilities and equipment.

A staff of eight permanent full-time, one permanent half-time, two career seasonals, and one temporary firefighter (Fig. 4) are currently allocated to Lower Suwannee National Wildlife Refuge (gray boxes). To accomplish the goals, objectives, and strategies outlined in this plan, additional staffing is needed. Five additional full-time permanent positions are required to fully implement this plan (white boxes). Additionally, two full-time positions willbe shared with Cedar Keys National Wildlife Refuge (white boxes with bold bordering). Finally, the current Assistant Refuge Manager position, GS-0485-5/7/9, will become a Refuge Operations Specialist position with the primary responsiblity of overseeing the daily operations of Cedar Keys Refuge. One of the identified new positions will be a Deputy Project Leader position, GS-0485-11/12, which would oversee staff and daily operations of Lower Suwannee Refuge.

If the Service is to succeed in the full implementation of this plan, base funding and minimum staffing must be increased. Along with base funding, maintenance funding must also increase so that the refuge may upgrade and improve facilities and equipment, as needed. Without the financial support from the U.S. Congress, Lower Suwannee National Wildlife Refuge will not be able to successfully manage habitat for threatened and endangered species and trust resources. The refuge will be unable to provide adequate environmental education and outreach. Wildlife-dependent recreational opportunities will be inadequate to meet the needs of society. Finally, the refuge will not endure as a unique resource for future generations.

## Resource Projects

The following projects directly support the refuge's goals and objectives. They do not necessarily fit under one goal, but rather support several goals.

**Figure 4. Organizational Chart for Lower Suwannee and Cedar Keys National Wildlife Refuges**

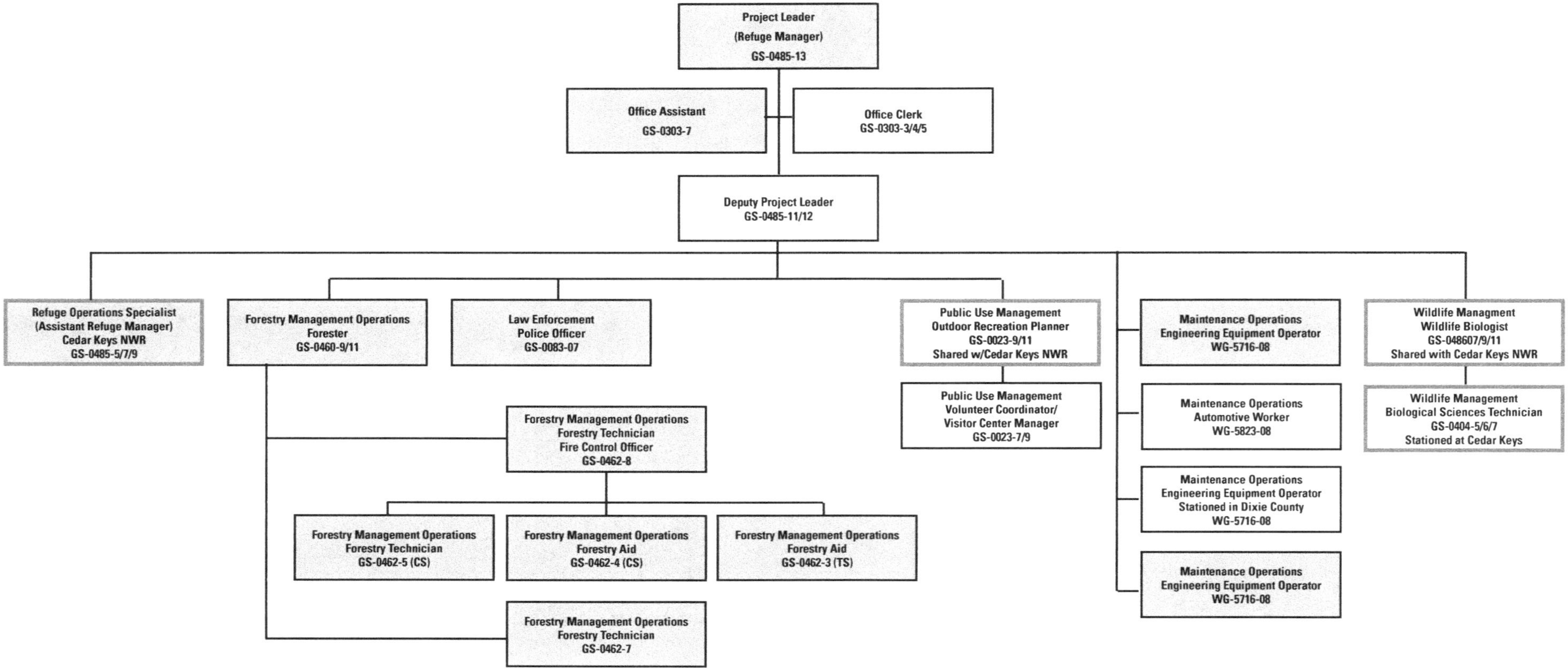

Project Leader
(Refuge Manager)
GS-0485-13

Office Clerk
GS-0303-3/4/5

Office Assistant
GS-0303-7

Deputy Project Leader
GS-0485-11/12

Refuge Operations Specialist
(Assistant Refuge Manager)
Cedar Keys NWR
GS-0485-5/7/9

Forestry Management Operations
Forester
GS-0460-9/11

Law Enforcement
Police Officer
GS-0083-07

Forestry Management Operations
Forestry Technician
Fire Control Officer
GS-0462-8

Forestry Management Operations
Forestry Technician
GS-0462-5 (CS)

Forestry Management Operations
Forestry Aid
GS-0462-4 (CS)

Forestry Management Operations
Forestry Technician
GS-0462-7

Forestry Management Operations
Forestry Aid
GS-0462-3 (TS)

Public Use Management
Outdoor Recreation Planner
GS-0023-9/11
Shared w/Cedar Keys NWR

Public Use Management
Volunteer Coordinator/
Visitor Center Manager
GS-0023-7/9

Maintenance Operations
Engineering Equipment Operator
WG-5716-08

Maintenance Operations
Automotive Worker
WG-5823-08

Maintenance Operations
Engineering Equipment Operator
Stationed in Dixie County
WG-5716-08

Maintenance Operations
Engineering Equipment Operator
WG-5716-08

Wildlife Managment
Wildlife Biologist
GS-048607/9/11
Shared with Cedar Keys NWR

Wildlife Management
Biological Sciences Technician
GS-0404-5/6/7
Stationed at Cedar Keys

Pine Plantation Burn
*USFWS Ken Litzenberger*

### Project 1

*Initial Base Funding* Additional base funding is needed to hire staff and cover normal, routine expenses. Five new full-time positions for Lower Suwannee National Wildlife Refuge and two new full-time positions to be shared with Cedar Keys National Wildlife Refuge are needed to meet minimum staffing needs. These positions will require equipment and transportation and will also affect utility expenses. The estimated costs for these new positions including salaries, benefits, and operations will total approximately $700,000 for the first year and $600,000 for recurring years.

### Project 2

*Administrative Facilities, Visitor's Services, and Education Center* Construction of a headquarter's facility is needed and will include a visitor center with interpretive displays and exhibits; a book store; an environmental education classroom; a large conference room; and six administrative offices. This facility, which will also serve Cedar Keys National Wildlife Refuge, will be in a location that supports both refuges and will serve large numbers of visitors. The construction cost will be approximately $2,000,000.

In lieu of a visitor center, a smaller administrative office and visitor contact station could be constructed. This facility could still support both refuges and have space for minor exhibits and a meeting room. The cost for this project will be approximately $400,000.

### Project 3

*Land Acquisition* This land acquisition project has two sections--inholdings and refuge expansion. Currently, 17 inholdings are within the approved refuge boundary (Fig. 5). Table 1 prioritizes the purchase of these lands if funding becomes available. If all the tracts were to be purchased, the cost will exceed $10,000,000.

The second part of the land acquisition project concerns the proposed expansion of the Lower Suwannee National Wildlife Refuge. In 1994, several tracts along the Suwannee River, outside the refuge's original acquisition boundary, were identified as nursery and spawning habitat for the endangered Gulf sturgeon. At that time, a Preliminary Project Proposal was conducted and followed with a Land Protection Plan and Environmental Assessment concerning this proposed expansion of the refuge. The project entered the Land Acquisition Priority System and was ranked number two in the country in 1996. It was not funded and in 2000 was ranked 84th in the country. The total acreage of the proposed acquisition is 9,970 acres with an estimated purchase cost of $15,000,000.

### Project 4

*Gopher Tortoise Population Study* The Gopher tortoise is a species of special concern in the State of Florida. As a keystone species for the sandy soil pine woods ecosystem, gopher tortoise absence can indicate a loss of suitable habitat or unfavorable management conditions. Gopher tortoise burrows serve a variety of other species. The absence of gopher tortoises in the ecosystem can have negative implications for rare, threatened and endangered species. Gopher tortoises are falling victim to a contagious respiratory disease that has the potential to adversely affect the species throughout its range. A study of the refuge's population will provide preliminary data, a population index, and determine the prevalence of the disease among this population. This study may also identify secondary burrow users, such as the endangered eastern indigo snake. The cost of the study is estimated at $80,000.

### Project 5

*Fire Effects Research* The refuge currently has an active fire management program. However, baseline information and post-burn vegetation analysis are needed to tailor the burn program to meet specific management

**LOWER
SUWANNEE
NATIONAL
WILDLIFE
REFUGE**

Comprehensive
Conservation
Plan

objectives. This project will initiate fire research on the effects of burning frequency, seasonality, and spatial distribution on the refuge's pine flatwoods, mixed cypress, and marsh ecosystems. Additionally, the refuge has large reptile and amphibian populations (e.g., the endangered eastern indigo snake and the gopher tortoise, a species of special concern). Basic research is needed to evaluate how prescribed fire parameters such as season, ignition methods and burn rotation affect refuge herpetofauna. This study will further investigate the impacts of prescribed fire on isolated wetlands. These wetlands may be maintained and possibly restored through the use of periodic prescribed fire to halt hardwood encroachment and succession. In many areas of Florida, fire was excluded from the isolated wetlands and, subsequently, suitable habitat for herpetofauna disappeared. The third treatment of this study will compare herpetofauna response in isolated wetlands where fire is used to those where fire has been excluded. The results from these three studies will provide information for managing habitats and wildlife populations on Lower Suwannee National Wildlife Refuge, tailor the forestry and fire management programs to meet specific habitat and population objectives, and provide valuable insight about herpetofauna which could be applied by other land managers. The cost of these research projects is estimated at $200,000.

### Project 6

*Dixie Compound Garage Facility and Crew Building* The Dixie County portion of the refuge is a 1-hour drive from the current headquarters. This portion of the refuge contains approximately 29,000 acres and 40 miles of roads. Equipment such as road graders, trucks, and bulldozers is stored in a pole shed located in the Dixie Compound. Presently, the refuge lacks a shop and a place to store tools. Additionally, a 1979 dilapidated mobile home is located in the compound. This structure was used as a sub-headquarters, crew room for staff, and temporary quarters for visiting researchers and volunteers. However, it is unsafe and an eyesore. A small garage with a tool room, crew room, and rest room facilities is needed. The cost of this project is estimated at $240,000.

### Project 7

*Enhance Resource Assessment through Geographic Information System* A Geographic Information System will permit refuge staff to digitize refuge habitats and incorporate biological, archaeological, and public use resources into databases. The refuge currently has a single-user GIS system and one GPS PLGR unit. A digitizer to capture fine scale data and a plotter for printing scales maps are necessary to have a fully functioning GIS system. The project will require new computer hardware, software, training, and a computer specialist to get the system up and running. The position will be a term position, not to exceed 4 years. This person will be required to train staff on how to use and maintain the system. The cost is estimated at $250,000.

Bird Watchers
*USFWS Ken Litzenberger*

Figure 5. Land Acquisition Map, Lower Suwannee National Wildlife Refuge

LOWER
SUWANNEE
NATIONAL
WILDLIFE
REFUGE

Comprehensive
Conservation
Plan

Table 1. Inholdings Within the Approved Boundary of Lower Suwannee National Wildlife Refuge

| TRACT | ACRES | ESTIMATED VALUE[1] | WILLING SELLER[2] |
|---|---|---|---|
| Asbell | 156 | 150,000 | yes |
| Drummond | 75 (2 parcels) | 40,000 | yes |
| Roe | 13 | 200,000 | no |
| Caber | 5295 | 8,000,000 | unknown |
| Sowell | 80 | 200,000 | unknown |
| Calton | 11 | 25,000 | no |
| Williams, et al. | 74 (camp cabin) | 500,000 | no |
| Hicks | 5 (home) | 200,000 | no |
| Osteen | 1 (home) | 75,000 | no |
| Abager | 91 | 300,000 | yes |
| Allen | 3 | 10,000 | unknown |
| Coon Island | <3 | 10,000 | yes |
| Yon | 30 (5 upland) | 50,000 | yes |
| Phillips | 79 | 150,000 | yes |
| Brown | 10 | 25,000 | yes |
| Batts | 72 | 150,000 | yes |
| Hudson | 65 | 25,000 | unknown |
| TOTALS | 6075 | 10,110,000 | |

[1]The estimated value figures are "best guess" estimates. Appraisals will be conducted to obtain fair market value prices. The Service is not allowed, by law, to pay above appraised value.

[2]The Service only acquires land from willing sellers.

Firefighter with Drip Torch
*USFWS Ken Litaenberger*

Project 8

*River Trail and Entrance Drive Enhancements* The entrance drive to the refuge, which leads to the administrative complex and an adjacent trail head area, is currently surfaced in limerock. This project proposes to resurface the 0.8-mile drive, the 500-square-foot trail head parking area, and the visitor contact station/administrative office parking lot. Additionally, the kiosk at the trail head is rotten and infested with termites. The information panels are outdated and in poor condition. The trail is approximately 0.5-mile in length with a 400-foot boardwalk and observation platform on the historic and beautiful Suwannee River. Approximately 10,000 people annually use this trail area. A new kiosk and interpretive panels are needed to replace the current structure and to highlight the trail improvements including the boardwalk and observation platform. The estimated costs of the entrance drive resurfacing, paving of two small parking lots, and replacing the information kiosk total $340,000.

Project 9

*Shell Mound Enhancements* The Shell Mound Unit of the refuge receives more than 50,000 visitors a year. Current public use amenities include a 1-mile, uninterpreted loop trail, a 0.3-mile loop trail with two information panels, a brochure box and small parking area at the trail heads, a small boat launching area, and a 400-foot disability accessible boardwalk and fishing pier. This project calls for the construction of two marsh boardwalks for the 1-mile trail. Currently, this trail is only fully accessible during low tide, as the marsh areas are wet during high tide. Additionally, an observation tower at Dennis Creek would greatly enhance the user's ability to observe wildlife and scenic vistas. The trail passes through unique coastal habitat and interpretive signs along the trail will educate visitors about the natural features found along the trail. On the Shell Mound Trail, two information panels are outdated and in poor condition. These panels would be replaced with new panels. In the parking area, the refuge sign and brochure box would be replaced with a 3-sided kiosk housing panels about the two trails, natural features and wildlife, for both Lower Suwannee and Cedar Keys Refuges. The estimated cost of this project is $50,000.

Sunset at Shell Mound
*USFWS Ken Sourbeer*

**Project 10**

*Develop Education Facilities* The Dixie County School District leases 16 acres of land near Fishborne Creek from the State of Florida which is surrounded by the refuge. The school district has plans to construct an environmental education facility on the property, but is short of funding. The Service needs to work cooperatively with the school district to apply for a grant to fund this project. The Service could help with the purchase of materials and provide construction supervision. The county could provide labor, probably from the correctional facility, to build a pole shed type structure. Grant money could be used to purchase a recycling, composting toilet for the site, while installation could also be by inmate labor with refuge supervision. The total estimated cost of the project is $20,000, with the Service's share being approximately $10,000, depending on funding or grant specifications.

**Project 11**

*Fire Equipment Storage and Cache* The original site plan for the administration area calls for an enclosed equipment building for vehicle storage. Presently, fire cache equipment is stored in several scattered locations due to space constraints. Additionally, equipment such as the engine, pumper unit, fire transport, and dozer are unprotected. This project will include the construction of an enclosed, 5-bay garage, with 4 bays for fire equipment storage and 1 bay for the fire cache. The estimated cost of this project is $300,000.

**Project 12**

*Shired Island Enhancements* Shired Island receives more than 40,000 visitors annually. The boat launch and parking area are in poor condition. This project will involve clearing and leveling the parking area and gravel resurfacing. The boat launch is eroding and needs bank stabilization. Currently, no signs or information panels for the refuge are located at this highly visited area. In addition to the parking area and launch improvements, a kiosk with refuge information and panels highlighting the unique natural features of the area will be constructed. The estimated cost of this project is $200,000.

**Project 13**

*Boundary Survey* Boundary surveys between refuge property and adjacent private property have not been conducted at several locations in Levy and Dixie Counties. These surveys were never conducted because the property was within the original acquisition boundary and it was assumed that these sites would eventually become part of the refuge. Several locations exist in both counties where the property remains in private ownership and the lack of a boundary line has caused management problems related to forest and fire management activities, public use, and law enforcement. Under this plan, the surveys will be conducted. The estimated cost for this project is $250,000.

Cypress Kness
*USFWS Jerry Gamble*

## Project 14

*Archaeological and Historical Survey* A comprehensive archaeological survey of the refuge is needed. The refuge contains archaeological sites that are more than 2000 years old. This project is necessary to identify, protect, and interpret the refuge's cultural resources. The estimated cost is $200,000.

## Project 15

*Replacement of Heavy Equipment* The refuge currently has two pieces of heavy equipment in need of replacement. The Fiat Allis crawler tractor was obtained by the Service in 1984, as used, excess property from the Army Corps of Engineers. This tractor is used to maintain 50 miles of road right-of-way. It is also used for land clearing, habitat management projects, and fire protection. A Champion brand motor grader, which is more than 20 years old, needs replacing. This grader was received by the refuge in 1979. The grader is used to maintain more than 50 miles of refuge roads for forestry and wildlife management, fire management and protection, and public access. The estimated replacement cost for both pieces of equipment is $325,000.

**Table 2. Funding Needs for Special Resource Projects of Lower Suwannee National Wildlife Refuge**

| PROJECTS | ONE TIME COST | FIRST YEAR NEED[1] | RECURRING BASE |
|---|---|---|---|
| 1. Initial Base Funding | | $700,000 | $600,000 |
| 2. Visitor Center et al. | $2,000,000 | | 50,000 |
| 3. Land Acquisition | 10,110,000 | | 75,000 |
| 4. Gopher Tortoise Study | | 80,000 | 5,000 |
| 5. Fire Effects | 200,000 | 100,000 | |
| 6. Garage and Crew Shop | 240,000 | | 5,000 |
| 7. GIS System | 250,000 | 100,000 | |
| 8. River Trail Projects | 340,000 | | 5,000 |
| 9. Shell Mound Projects | 50,000 | | |
| 10. Education Facilities | 10,000 | | |
| 11. Fire Equipment Storage | 300,000 | | 5,000 |
| 12. Shired Island Projects | 200,000 | | 5,000 |
| 13. Boundary Survey | 250,000 | | 5,000 |
| 14. Archaeological Survey | 200,000 | | 5,000 |
| 15. Heavy Equipment | 325,000 | | |
| TOTAL | 14,475,000 | 980,000 | 760,000 |

[1]First year need for these projects is included in the one time cost figure.

## Volunteers

Volunteer assistance to the refuge has been valuable, particularly in the area of public use. Lower Suwannee Refuge has a small, but dedicated corps of volunteers. One volunteer works more than 200 hours annually at Shell Mound maintaining the trails and collecting litter. He has also assisted with the construction of a boardwalk and a kiosk. Several volunteers assist with data entry and other office work. Other volunteers lead nature walks, canoe tours, wildflower walks, and birding trips for special refuge events such as National Wildlife Refuge Week, and assist in staffing festival exhibits. Still others assist with colonial bird, shorebird, and migratory bird surveys. Volunteers contribute approximately 1,000 hours annually to refuge projects.

**LOWER
SUWANNEE
NATIONAL
WILDLIFE
REFUGE**

Comprehensive
Conservation
Plan

Volunteers will continue to play an integral role in assisting staff with fulfilling the mission and vision of this refuge. The current limiting factor in volunteer recruitment is not a lack of community interest, but the lack of staff to nurture and oversee this program. The development of a "Friends" group will provide interested citizens with an outlet to become more involved. However, this program will not fully develop without a staff person to make this dream a reality.

### Monitoring and Evaluation

Extensive research and monitoring of natural resources will occur once this plan is implemented and minimum staffing needs are met. This knowledge will give refuge managers and staff specialists the data to judge how habitat management has impacted refuge resources. A major objective of the investigations is not only to provide information to local managers, but to provide a database which will benefit other land managers with similar resources.

This plan will be augmented with detailed step-down management plans to address management actions in support of refuge goals and objectives, and to implement the identified strategies. Annual work guidance and the Maintenance Management System and Refuge Operational Needs System are the annual mechanisms for requesting funding and accounting for completion of the objectives, strategies, and projects identified in the plan. It will be reviewed every 5 years to determine if these goals and objectives are being met and if different strategies are needed to assist the refuge in moving towards fulfilling its vision. Public involvement in the evaluation process and in plan implementation will be encouraged.